The Riverside
IN CROSS STITCH

Shirley Watts

MEREHURST

For my Aunty Jessie and Uncle Ron – with love

THE CHARTS

Some of the designs in this book are very detailed and due to inevitable space limitations, the charts may be shown on a comparatively small scale; in such cases, readers may find it helpful to have the particular chart with which they are currently working enlarged.

THREADS

The projects in this book were all stitched with DMC stranded cotton embroidery threads. The keys given with each chart also list thread combinations for those who wish to use Anchor or Madeira threads. It should be pointed out that the shades produced by different companies vary slightly, and it is not always possible to find identical colours in a different range.

First published in 1996 by Merehurst Limited
Ferry House, 51-57 Lacy Road, Putney, London SW15 1PR
Photography and illustrations copyright © 1996 Merehurst Limited
Text and charts copyright © 1996 Shirley Watts
ISBN 1 85391 511 4

A catalogue record for this book is available from the British Library.

Edited by Diana Lodge
Designed by Maggie Aldred
Photography by Juliet Piddington
Illustrations by John Hutchinson
Typesetting by Dacorum Type & Print, Hemel Hempstead
Colour separation by Fotographics Limited, UK – Hong Kong
Printed in Hong Kong by Wing King Tong

Merehurst is the leading publisher of craft books and has an excellent range of titles to suit all levels. Please send to the address above for our free catalogue, stating the title of this book.

CONTENTS

INTRODUCTION

Rivers have a universal appeal, largely because of the diversity of environments they provide for wildlife and the fascination that water holds for all of us – old and young alike.

Many of the projects I have included in this book are small ones that can be completed in a few evenings by those with only a little experience of cross stitch – greetings cards, a bookmark and a small trinket box, as well as one or two more unusual projects, such as a fisherman's mug and a postage stamp book. For those who prefer larger projects there are pictures, book jackets and napkins.

With a little imagination all the designs can be used in different ways. Small motifs may be extracted from bigger designs to mount in small projects. More experienced cross stitchers may like to work the designs on different counts from those suggested – to suit their eye-sight; but in this case it is important to calculate the size of the completed design before beginning. However large or small your project, you will find that only full cross stitches are used and back-stitching is kept to a minimum – added only to highlight a feature or emphasize an otherwise indistinct line.

I hope that you will enjoy stitching these designs. Whether you are a wild flower enthusiast, an ornithologist, a fisherman, a rambler or someone who simply enjoys 'messing about on the river,' I hope that you will find something here to appeal to you.

Happy stitching!

BASIC SKILLS

BEFORE YOU BEGIN

PREPARING THE FABRIC
Even with an average amount of handling, many evenweave fabrics tend to fray at the edges, so it is a good idea to overcast the raw edges, using ordinary sewing thread, before you begin.

FABRIC
Most of the projects in this book use Aida fabric, which is ideal both for beginners and more advanced stitchers as it has a surface of clearly designated squares, each cross stitch being worked over a square. Other projects use perforated paper, specially produced for counted thread embroidery, and evenweave Jobelan fabric; the latter has 28 threads per 2.5cm (1in) each way, but stitches are worked over two threads. All evenweaves have a count, referring to the number of Aida blocks, threads or perforations per 2.5cm (1in) in each direction. The lower the count, therefore, the larger the finished stitching. If you wish to use fabric with a different stitch count, count the maximum number of stitches on the chart horizontally and vertically and divide these numbers by the stitch count of your chosen fabric; this will give you the dimensions of the design when stitched on your fabric.

THE INSTRUCTIONS
Each project begins with a full list of the materials that you will require. The measurements given for the embroidery fabric include a minimum of 5cm (2in) all around to allow for stretching it in a frame and preparing the edges to prevent them from fraying.

Colour keys for stranded embroidery cottons – DMC, Anchor or Madeira – are given with each chart. It is assumed that you will need to buy one skein of each colour mentioned in a particular key, even though you may use less, but where two or more skeins are needed, this information is included in the main list of requirements.

Before you begin to embroider, always mark the centre of the design with two lines of basting stitches, one vertical and one horizontal, running from edge to edge of the fabric, as indicated by the arrows on the charts.

As you stitch, use the centre lines given on the chart and the basting threads on your fabric as reference points for counting the squares and threads to position your design accurately.

WORKING IN A HOOP

A hoop is the most popular frame for use with small areas of embroidery. It consists of two rings, one fitted inside the other; the outer ring usually has an adjustable screw attachment so that it can be tightened to hold the stretched fabric in place. Hoops are available in several sizes, ranging from 10cm (4in) in diameter to quilting hoops with a diameter of 38cm (15in). Hoops with table stands or floor stands attached are also available.

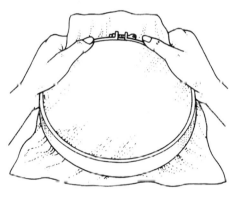

1 To stretch your fabric in a hoop, place the area to be embroidered over the inner ring and press the outer ring over it, with the tension screw released. Tissue paper can be placed between the outer ring and the embroidery, so that the hoop does not mark the fabric. Lay the tissue paper over the fabric when you set it in the hoop, then tear away the central embroidery area.

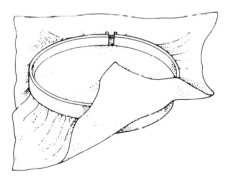

2 Smooth the fabric and, if necessary, straighten the grain before tightening the screw. The fabric should be evenly stretched.

WORKING IN A RECTANGULAR FRAME

Rectangular frames are more suitable for larger pieces of embroidery. They consist of two rollers, with tapes attached, and two flat side pieces, which slot into the rollers and are held in place by pegs or screw attachments. Available in different sizes, either alone or with adjustable table or floor stands, frames are measured by the length of the roller tape, and range in size from 30cm (12in) to 68cm (27in).

As alternatives to a slate frame, canvas stretchers and the backs of old picture frames can be used. Provided there is sufficient extra fabric around the finished size of the embroidery, the edges can be turned under and simply attached with drawing pins (thumb tacks) or staples.

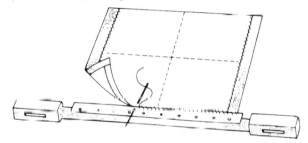

1 To stretch your fabric in a rectangular frame, cut out the fabric, allowing at least an extra 5cm (2in) all around the finished size of the embroidery. Baste a single 12mm (½in) turning on the top and bottom edges and oversew strong tape, 2.5cm (1in) wide, to the other two sides. Mark the centre line both ways with basting stitches. Working from the centre outward and using strong thread, oversew the top and bottom edges to the roller tapes. Fit the side pieces into the slots, and roll any extra fabric on one roller until the fabric is taut.

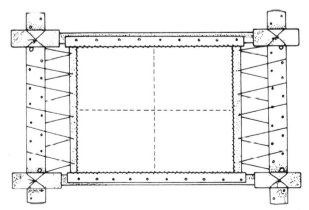

2 Insert the pegs or adjust the screw attachments to secure the frame. Thread a large-eyed needle (chenille needle) with strong thread or fine string

5

and lace both edges, securing the ends around the intersections of the frame. Lace the webbing at 2.5cm (1in) intervals, stretching the fabric evenly.

EXTENDING EMBROIDERY FABRIC

It is easy to extend a piece of embroidery fabric, such as a bookmark, to stretch it in a hoop.

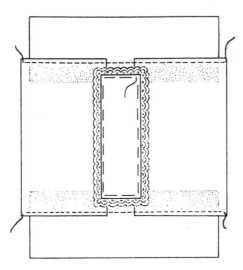

● Fabric oddments of a similar weight can be used. Simply cut four pieces to size (in other words, to the measurement that will fit both the embroidery fabric and your hoop) and baste them to each side of the embroidery fabric before stretching it in the hoop in the usual way.

THE STITCHES

CROSS STITCH

For all cross stitch embroidery, the following two methods of working are used. In each case, neat rows of vertical stitches are produced on the back of the fabric.

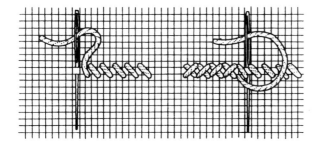

● When stitching large areas, work in horizontal rows. Working from right to left, complete the first row of evenly spaced diagonal stitches over the number of threads specified in the project instructions. Then, working from left to right, repeat the process. Continue in this way, making sure each stitch crosses in the same direction.

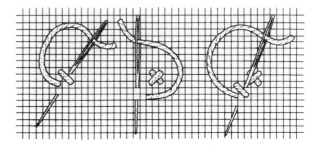

● When stitching diagonal lines, work downwards, completing each stitch before moving to the next. When starting a project always begin to embroider at the centre of the design and work outwards to ensure that the design will be placed centrally on the fabric.

BACKSTITCH

Backstitch is used in the projects to give emphasis to a particular foldline, an outline or a shadow. The stitches are worked over the same number of threads as the cross stitch, forming continuous straight or diagonal lines.

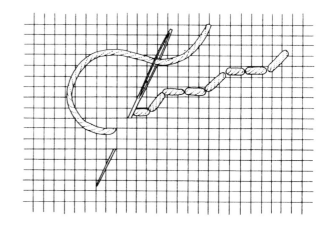

● Make the first stitch from left to right; pass the needle behind the fabric and bring it out one stitch length ahead to the left. Repeat and continue in this way along the line.

HEMSTITCH

Remove a single thread from the fabric at the hemline (the start of the fringe). Bring the needle out on the right side, two threads below the drawn-thread line. Working from left to right, pick up either two or three threads, as shown in the diagram. Bring the needle out again and insert it behind the fabric, to emerge two threads down, ready to make the next stitch. Before reinserting the needle, pull the thread tight, so that the bound threads form a neat group. To complete the fringe, remove the weft threads below the hemstitching.

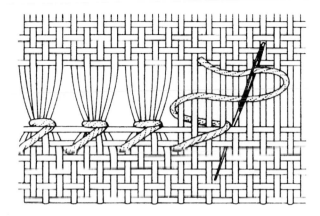

If you wish to make your own napkins and finish them with a fringed edge, you can either secure the fringe with machine zig zag stitching or with a traditional hemstitch finish.

THREADING TECHNIQUES FOR BLENDING FILAMENT

You should use no more than 45cm (18in) of thread at a time. Double the thread about 5cm (2in) at one end, and inset the loop through the eye of the needle. Pull the loop over the point of the needle and gently pull the loop towards the end of the eye to secure the thread to the needle. If you are using a combination of blending filament and stranded cotton, thread the latter through the eye in the usual way, and clip it to match the length of the blending filament.

Kreinik threads are available from an increasing number of needlework shops, but if you have problems see page 40 for mail-order suppliers.

MOUNTING EMBROIDERY

The cardboard should be cut to the size of the finished embroidery, with an extra 6mm (¼in) added all round to allow for the recess in the frame.

LIGHTWEIGHT FABRICS

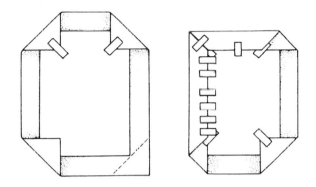

1 Place embroidery face down, with the cardboard centred on top, and basting and pencil lines matching. Begin by folding over the fabric at each corner and securing it with masking tape.

2 Working first on one side and then the other, fold over the fabric on all sides and secure it firmly with pieces of masking tape, placed about 2.5cm (1in) apart. Also neaten the mitred corners with masking tape, pulling the fabric tightly to give a firm, smooth finish.

HEAVIER FABRICS

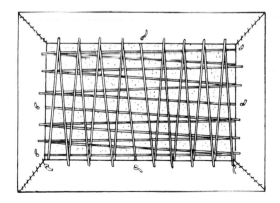

● Lay the embroidery face down, with the cardboard centred on top; fold over the edges of the fabric on opposite sides, making mitred folds at the corners, and lace across, using strong thread. Repeat on the other two sides. Finally, pull up the fabric firmly over the cardboard. Overstitch the mitred corners.

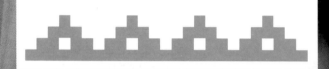

River Scene

In the cool clear light of a summer
morning, the grey heron stands
motionless in shallow waters by the
river's edge. The watchful bird waits
patiently for a fish to surface –
a potential meal for a hungry bird.
The subtle colours offer an enjoyable
challenge to the stitcher.

RIVER SCENE

YOU WILL NEED

For the picture, mounted in a rectangular landscape frame, with a coloured mount 4cm (1½in) deep, with an aperture measuring 22.5cm × 18cm (8¾in × 7 in):

40.5cm × 38cm (16in × 15in) of pale blue, 14-count Aida fabric
Stranded embroidery cotton in the colours given in the panel
No24 tapestry needle
Strong thread for lacing across the back when mounting
Stiff cardboard for backing
Frame of your choice
Mount to fit the frame, with an aperture as specified above

•

THE EMBROIDERY

Prepare the fabric by marking the centre lines of the design with basting stitches. Start your embroidery from the centre of the design, completing the cross stitching first, and then the backstitching. Use three strands of thread for the cross stitches and two strands for the backstitching. Leaving the basting stitches in place, gently steam press the finished embroidery on the wrong side.

ASSEMBLING THE PICTURE

Using the basting stitches as guidelines, centre the picture over the cardboard mount, which should be cut to the size of the chosen frame. Lace the embroidery over the mount, following the instructions on page 7, and remove basting stitches. Insert the coloured mount into the frame and then the mounted embroidery; complete assembly of the frame according to the manufacturer's instructions.

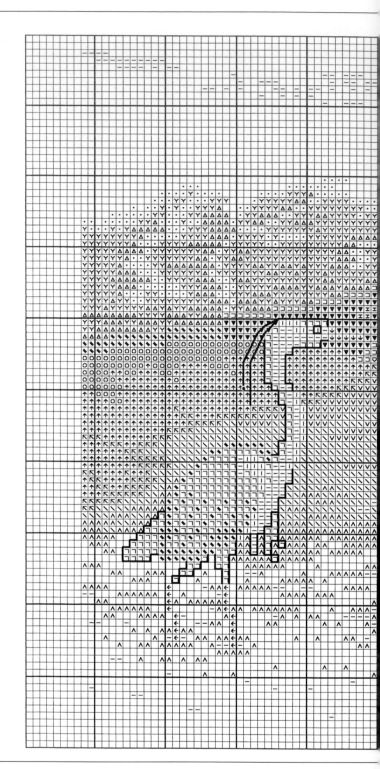

GREY HERON								
(Ardea cinerea)		DMC	ANCHOR	MADEIRA				
⊠	Medium grey	414	400	1801	◥	Light grey blue	932	920	1710
⊓	Pale grey	415	398	1803	∧	Pale blue	928	274	1709
⊟	White	White	1	White	↓	Orange	720	326	0309
⊡	Black	310	403	Black	←	Light orange	722	323	0307
1	Dark fawn	840	379	1912	O	Dull green	3052	859	1509
2	Fawn	842	376	1910	△	Dark green	3362	862	1601
5	Yellow	743	297	0113	Y	Green	3363	861	1602
V	Grey blue	931	921	1711	·	Light green	3364	843	1603

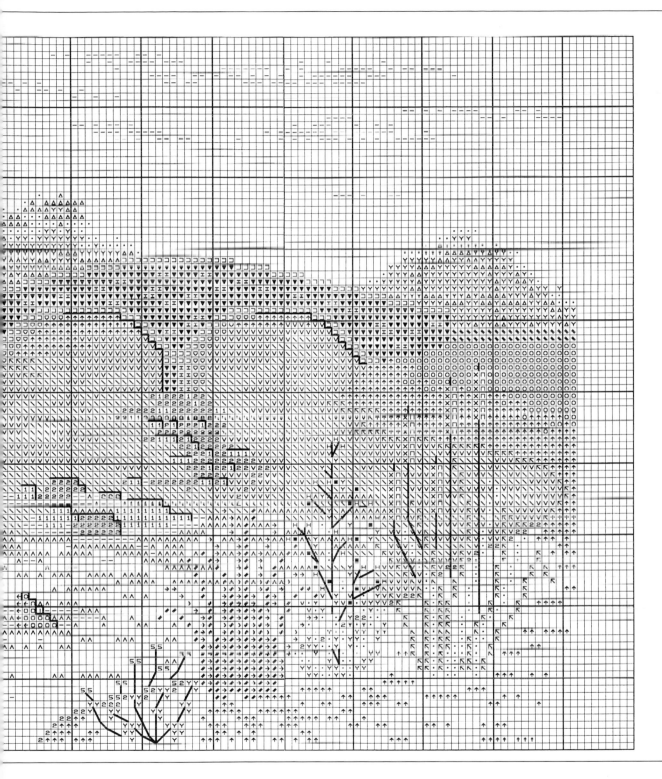

		DMC	ANCHOR	MADEIRA
⟋	Bluish green	320	215	1311
⟍	Dark dull green	3051	846	1508
→	Dark blue green	319	246	1313
↑	Light dull green	3053	859	1510
♡	Dark grey	413	401	1713
⊓	Brown	898	360	2006
X	Reddish brown	433	371	2008
⊐	Mushroom	451	233	1808

		DMC	ANCHOR	MADEIRA
⊥	Light mushroom	452	232	1807
▼	Pale mushroom	453	231	1806
H	Deep pink	602	63	0702
■	Pink	603	62	0701

Note: backstitch the eye of the heron in orange; the fish's head and the flower stems in dark green; the heron's crest and the fish's mouth in black; the bullrush stalks in brown; the detail on the rocks, the bridge arches and the heron's head, neck and body in dark grey, and the fish's eye in yellow.

Fisherman's Log Book and Mug

Two ideal gifts for an angler —
a special log book in which to record
catches, and a large mug from which
to sip a warming brew, as he waits
for that 'really big one'.

FISHERMAN'S LOG BOOK AND MUG

YOU WILL NEED

For the log book, measuring 21.5cm × 15.5cm (8½in × 6in):

53cm × 30.5cm (21in × 12in) of cream, 18-count Aida fabric
47cm × 16.5cm (18½in × 6½in) of white interfacing
Stranded embroidery cotton in the colours given in the appropriate panel
No26 tapestry needle
A notebook of your choice

For the fisherman's mug, height 10cm (4in), diameter 8.5cm (3½in):

Stranded embroidery cotton in the colours given in the appropriate panel
No24 tapestry needle
Mug, available from needlework stockists complete with ready-cut piece of 14-count canvas (for suppliers, see page 40)

•

THE LOG BOOK

Fold the Aida in half, giving you a working area of 26.5cm × 30.5cm (10½in × 12in). With the fold on the left, measure in 12mm (½in) and baste from top to bottom. From this line, measure a further 15.5cm (6in) across and baste another, parallel line. Baste two horizontal lines 21.5cm (8½in) apart, equidistant from the top and bottom edges of your working area, leaving a rectangular area measuring 21.5cm × 15.5cm (8½in × 6in) for the front cover of your log book. Centre your embroidery in this area. Starting from the centre, use two strands of cotton for the cross stitching, and two for backstitching. Steam press on the wrong side when complete.

Centre the interfacing on the Aida and fold in a narrow hem along all the edges, enclosing the interfacing. Machine stitch into position. Centre the book on the wrong side of the fabric and fold the extra width over the front and back side edges of the cover. Topstitch through the folds at the top and bottom to form pockets.

THE MUG

For the mug, find the centre of the canvas and start your embroidery from the centre of the design. Complete the cross stitching first, using three strands of thread and then the backstitching, using two.

Assemble the mug, following the manufacturer's instructions.

PERCH AND ROACH MUG ▼ *(Perca fluviatilis & Rutilus rutilus)*		DMC	ANCHOR	MADEIRA
⊠	Black	310	403	Black
⊟	Cream	712	387	2101
⊡	Dark grey	844	1041	1810
6	Greeny yellow	734	280	1610
8	Grey blue	930	922	1712
T	Blue	932	920	1710
⊠	Pale blue	928	274	1709
⊠	Pale grey	762	397	1804
●	Deep pink	351	11	0214
⊥	Pink	352	9	0303
+	Orange	720	326	0309
Y	Light green	772	264	1604
⊓	Grey	645	273	1811
⊥	Brown yellow	834	874	2204
■	Pale pink	225	892	0814
	Yellow*	972	298	0107
	White*	White	1	White

Note: backstitch the eyes in yellow; the fins, gills, mouths and bubbles in dark grey; and the eye highlights in white* (starred colours are used for backstitching only).*

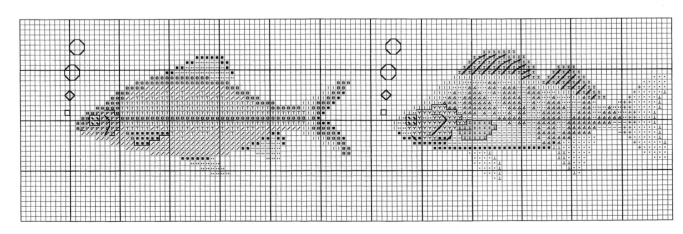

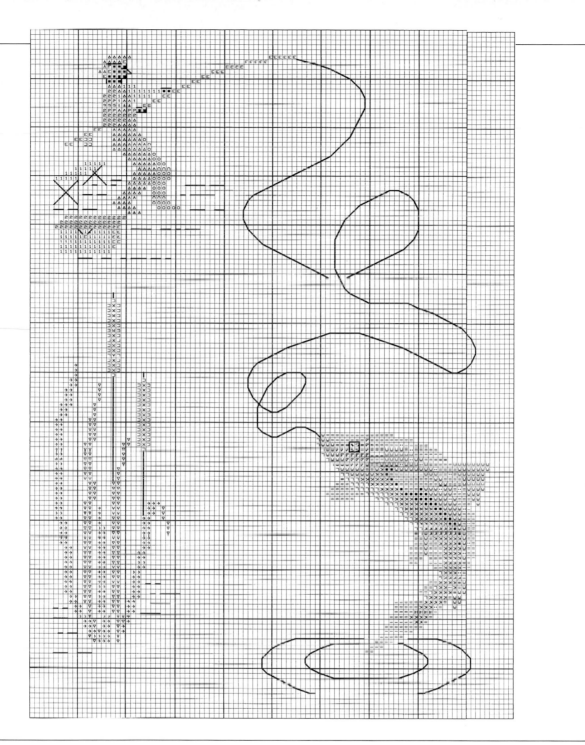

SALMON LOG BOOK ▲
(Salmo salar)

		DMC	ANCHOR	MADEIRA
⊠	Black	310	403	Black
⊐	Pale grey blue	928	274	1709
E	Dark brown	3031	905	2003
1	Ginger brown	680	901	2210
2	Gold	676	891	2208
5	Deep yellow	972	298	0107
=	Dark grey blue	924	851	1706
⊍	Grey blue	926	850	1707
⋊	Light grey blue	927	849	1708
▽	Pale grey	762	397	1804
▽	Dark green	520	862	1514
○	Dull green	3362	263	1601

		DMC	ANCHOR	MADEIRA
△	Light green	522	859	1513
→	Green	3363	261	1602
⏛	Dark grey	844	1041	1810
X	Reddish brown	433	371	2008
⊐	Brown	898	360	2006
■	Pale pink	225	892	0814
	Pale blue*	775	128	1001

Note: backstitch the fish's eye in deep yellow; the fishing line, and the detail on man's hands and face in dark grey; the water in pale blue* (used for backstitching only); the ground around the rushes and around the man in dark green; and the bullrush stems and detail on the basket and seat in dark brown.

Duck Napkins

Ducks have a universal appeal.
The elegant and attractive pintail is
largely a winter visitor; the teal
is with us all year and is Britain's
smallest duck, while the larger
shelduck is found most often on the
tidal estuaries of rivers.

DUCK NAPKINS

YOU WILL NEED

For each napkin, measuring 38cm (15in) square:

38cm (15in) square of grey, 28-count Jobelan fabric
(No429.79)
Stranded embroidery cotton in the colours given
in the appropriate panel
No26 tapestry needle

●

THE EMBROIDERY

Baste a vertical line 6cm (2¼in) in from the left-hand side, and a horizontal one 6cm (2¼in) up from the lower edge. The point where these two lines intersect is the bottom left-hand corner of a 13cm (5in) square which will hold your chosen duck motif. Complete this square with basting stitches, and then find the centre point. Start your embroidery from the stitch nearest to this point. Care must be taken in counting, as you will be working over two fabric threads. Use two strands of cotton in the needle for both cross stitch and backstitch, except when back-stitching beaks and eye highlights, where one strand is used. Complete all the cross stitching before adding the backstitches. Gently steam press the finished embroidery on the wrong side.

FRINGING

On all four sides of your napkin, withdraw a single fabric thread 12mm (½in) in from the outer edge. The fringing can be secured in one of several ways: by machining around the square left by the withdrawn threads, using either straight stitch or narrow zigzag stitch, or by overcasting every alternate thread by hand.

When you have secured the line by your chosen method, remove all cross threads below the stitched line to complete the fringe. Alternatively, if a more hard-wearing edge is preferred, a folded and stitched hem can be used instead of fringing.

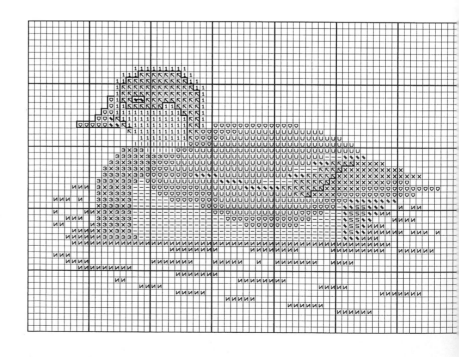

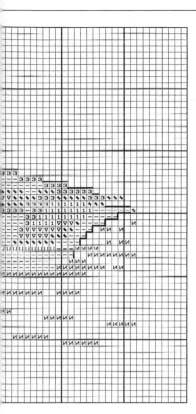

SHELDUCK ◀
(Tadorna tadorna)

		DMC	ANCHOR	MADEIRA
◩	Black	310	403	Black
⊟	Ecru	Ecru	926	Ecru
1	Ginger	435	365	2010
2	Light ginger	436	363	2011
3	Oatmeal	543	276	1909
Ͷ	Grey blue	926	850	1707
Ͷ	Red	347	13	0407
▽	Dark green	934	862	1506
▬	Green	936	269	1507
U	Fawn	842	376	1910

Note: backstitch the body of the duck in fawn, and the eye in ecru.

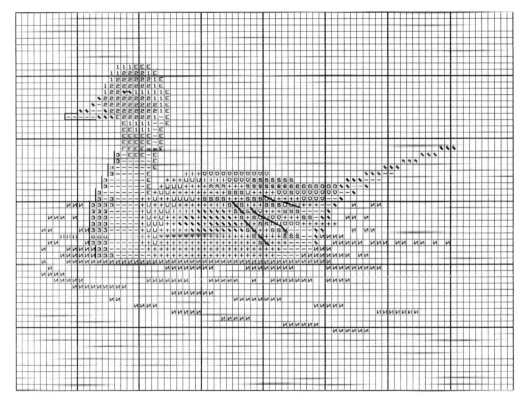

TEAL ◀
(Anas crecca)

		DMC	ANCHOR	MADEIRA
◩	Black	310	403	Black
⊟	Ecru	Ecru	926	Ecru
I	Chestnut	434	309	2009
1	Ginger	435	365	2010
3	Oatmeal	543	276	1909
5	Lemon	727	293	0110
Ͷ	Grey blue	926	850	1707
◸	Green	937	268	1504
X	Light brown	840	379	1912
▽	Fawn	642	392	1906
U	Light fawn	613	956	2109

Note: backstitch the beak of the duck in black, and the nostril, eye, head and wing in ecru.

PINTAIL ▲
(Anas acuta)

		DMC	ANCHOR	MADEIRA
◩	Black	310	403	Black
⊟	Ecru	Ecru	926	Ecru
E	Chestnut	434	309	2009
1	Ginger	435	365	2010
2	Light ginger	436	363	2011
3	Oatmeal	543	276	1909
Ͷ	Grey blue	926	850	1707
S	Brown	839	380	1913
♡	Light brown	840	379	1912
+	Fawny brown	841	378	1911
U	Fawn	842	376	1910

Note: backstitch the duck's breast in fawn; the beak and wing feathers in black, and the eye highlight in ecru.

Frame and Trinket Box

Beside undisturbed lowland river banks, the water vole *(Arvicola terrestris)* spends its day feeding on waterside plants, swimming along the edge of the river or making its burrows near the bank.

FRAME AND TRINKET BOX

YOU WILL NEED

For the frame, measuring 27cm × 22cm
(10³⁄₄in × 8³⁄₄in) internally with an aperture
measuring 14cm × 9cm (5¹⁄₂in × 3¹⁄₂in):

*27cm × 22cm (10³⁄₄in × 8³⁄₄in) of white,
14-count perforated paper
Stranded embroidery cotton in the colours given
in the appropriate panel
No24 tapestry needle
27cm x 22cm (10³⁄₄in × 8³⁄₄in) of iron-on interfacing
Frame of your choice*

For the trinket box, with a lid measuring 7.5cm (3in)
in diameter:

*12.5cm (5in) square of cream, 18-count Aida fabric
12.5cm (5in) square of iron-on interfacing
Standard embroidery cotton in the colours given in
the appropriate panel
No26 tapestry needle
Trinket box (for suppliers, see page 40)*

Note: Trinket boxes are available with bowls
made from wood, hand-cut crystal, silver-plate or
porcelain in a variety of colours. You may wish to
choose a bowl to match one of the colours
in the embroidery.

•

THE EMBROIDERY

For the frame, find the centre of the perforated paper
by counting the spaces between the holes. Mark this
point with a soft pencil, and then count out to a
convenient starting point on the border. Complete all
the cross stitches first, and then add the backstitching. Use three strands of embroidery cotton in the
needle for the cross stitching and two strands for the
backstitching.

For the trinket box, find the centre point on your
square of Aida and, beginning from the centre of the
pattern, embroider the motif, using two strands of
cotton in the needle for the cross stitches and for
backstitching in green. For the more delicate
backstitched features, use only one thread. When
complete, steam press on the wrong side.

MOUNTING AND ASSEMBLY

For the frame, use a soft pencil to mark the position
of the aperture which will display your photograph or
picture. Cut this out, using a sharp craft knife. Iron
the interfacing to the back of the embroidered
perforated paper, and then use the craft knife to trim
the backed perforated paper to fit your chosen frame,
and to remove the interfacing from the aperture.
Insert the embroidered paper into your frame.

For the trinket box, iron the interfacing to the
back of the embroidery. Take the acetate inset from
the lid of your bowl and place it over the embroidery.
This will enable you to centre the motif within the
circular space available. Using the acetate as a
template, draw around it with a soft pencil. Cut
around the circle with a sharp pair of scissors, and
follow the manufacturer's instructions to complete
the assembly.

WATER VOLE BOX ▼			
(Arvicola terrestris)	DMC	ANCHOR	MADEIRA
⊠ Black	310	403	Black
⧄ Dark brown	3021	382	1904
③ Cream	3047	886	2205
∩ Deep pink	3607	87	0708
⊥ Dusky pink	224	893	0813
⧅ Dark green	3362	862	1601
→ Green	3363	861	1602
▮▮ Brown	610	889	2106
⊓ Fawn	612	832	2108
· Pink	3608	86	0709
■ Pale pink	3609	85	0710
Ecru*	Ecru	926	Ecru

*Note: backstitch the vole's whiskers in dark brown; the eye highlight
in ecru* (used for backstitching only); the flower stalk and sepals in
green; the vole's front in brown; the vole's ear in cream, and the eye
outline in black.*

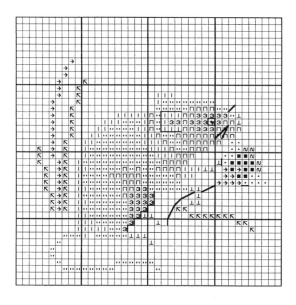

WATER VOLE ▲	DMC	ANCHOR	MADEIRA
◩ Black	310	403	Black
⊟ Ecru	Ecru	926	Ecru
⊡ Dark brown	3021	382	1904
③ Cream	3047	886	2205
ℕ Deep pink	3607	87	0708
⊥ Dusky pink	224	893	0813
◩ Dark green	3362	862	1601
⌐ Green	3363	861	1602
↑ Light green	3364	260	1603
▮▮ Brown	610	889	2106
⊓ Fawn	612	832	2108
· Pink	3608	86	0709
■ Pale pink	3609	85	0710

Note: backstitch the vole's whiskers and the flower stamens in dark brown; the vole's eye highlight in ecru; the flower stalks and sepals in green; the vole's front in brown; the vole's ear in cream, and the eye outline in black.

Greetings Cards

As you sit quietly by the riverside on a summer's day, you may observe the small brown dipper bobbing up and down searching for water insects, the swallow catching its food on the wing, or even the vivid colours of the kingfisher.

GREETINGS CARDS

YOU WILL NEED

For either the Kingfisher or the Dipper card, each measuring 20cm × 15cm (8in × 6in), with an oval cut-out measuring 14.5cm × 9.5cm (5³⁄₄in × 3³⁄₄in), or for the Swallow card, measuring 20cm × 15.5cm (8in × 6¹⁄₄in), with a cut-out measuring 12.5cm (5in) square:

20cm × 15cm (8in × 6in) of cream,
18-count Aida fabric
20cm × 15cm (8in × 6in) of iron-on interfacing
Stranded embroidery cotton and blending filament in the colours given in the appropriate panel
No26 tapestry needle
Greetings card (for suppliers, see page 40)

•

THE EMBROIDERY

For each card, find the centre of your piece of Aida, and start your embroidery from the centre of the design. Work all the cross stitches first and then add the backstitching. Use two strands of cotton for the cross stitch, except where a metallic thread is indicated. In this case, use one strand of cotton together with one strand of metallic thread. For the backstitching, use one strand of cotton. Gently steam press on the wrong side when complete.

SWALLOW ▶ (*Hirundo rustica*)	DMC	ANCHOR	MADEIRA
⊠ Black	310	403	Black
⊓ Pale grey	415	398	1803
⊟ White	White	1	White
1 Dark orange	920	339	0312
2 Orange	921	349	0311
= Navy	939	127	1009
C Light iridescent blue	775	128	1001
Kr. 001 (Kreinik silver blending filament)			
⟋ Dark grey blue	930	922	1712
⋈ Grey blue	931	921	1711
∧ Light grey blue	932	920	1710
+ Pale orange	722	323	0307
X Cream	712	387	2101
▽ Fawn	613	956	2109
⊟ Grey	413	401	1713
▲ Light navy	823	150	1008

Note: backstitch the eye highlight in white; the fly in black; the tail in navy; the edge of the wing in fawn, and the eye outline in pale grey.

ASSEMBLING THE CARDS

Iron the interfacing to the back of the embroidery, and trim both to measure about 12mm (¹⁄₂in) larger all around than the cut-out window.

Open out the self-adhesive mount and centre the embroidery behind the aperture. Fold the card and press firmly to secure. Some cards may require a dab of glue to ensure a secure and neat finish.

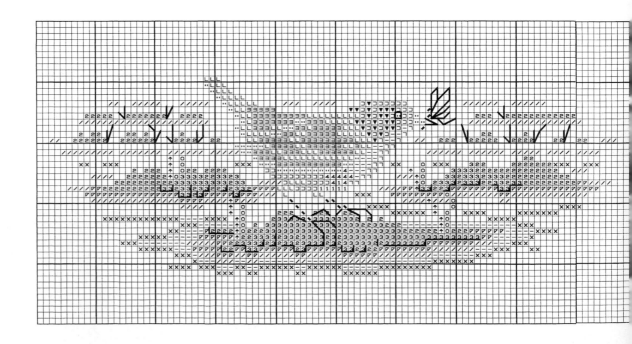

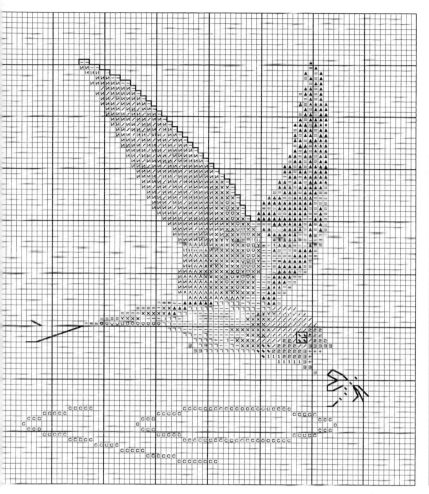

KINGFISHER ▼
(*Alcedo atthis*)

		DMC	ANCHOR	MADEIRA
⊓	Pale grey	415	398	1803
−	White	White	1	White
∣	Dull orange	922	1003	0310
4	Light orange	977	1002	2301
=	Dark blue grey	924	851	1706
S	Blue	797	132	0912
+	Green	991	189	1204
⋉	Iridescent blue	597	168	1110
	+ *Kr. 006 (Kreinik blue blending filament)*			
C	Turquoise	597	168	1110
U	Light turquoise	598	167	1111
╱	Dark grey	413	401	1713
∧	Light iridescent blue	775	128	1001
	+ *Kr. 001 (Kreinik silver blending filament)*			
⊥	Dark orange	900	333	0208
+	Orange	721	324	0308
▮▮	Black	310	403	Black
∠	Grey blue	926	850	1707
X	Pale orange	402	347	2307
V	Fawn	422	372	2102

Note: backstitch the eye highlight in white, and the eye outline in pale grey.

DIPPER ◄
(*Cinclus cinclus*)

		DMC	ANCHOR	MADEIRA
◲	Grey	413	401	1713
⊓	Pale grey	415	398	1803
−	White	White	1	White
1	Rust	301	349	2306
2	Dark fawn	1140	379	1912
3	Fawn	842	376	1910
4	Orange	721	324	0308
X	Blue	794	175	0907
╱	Pale blue	775	128	1001
▽	Silvery white	White	1	White
	+ *Kr. 001 (Kreinik silver blending filament)*			
O	Dark green	3345	268	1406
⌀	Yellowy green	581	266	1609
↑	Green	3347	267	1408
▮▮	Very dark brown	3371	382	2004
∟	Dark brown	3031	905	2003
⊒	Brown	610	889	2106
⊔	Yellow brown	829	906	2113
▼	Light brown	420	375	2104

Note: backstitch the fly, the beak and detail on the rocks in very dark brown; the birds feet in grey; the grass between the rocks in green, and the eye in pale grey.

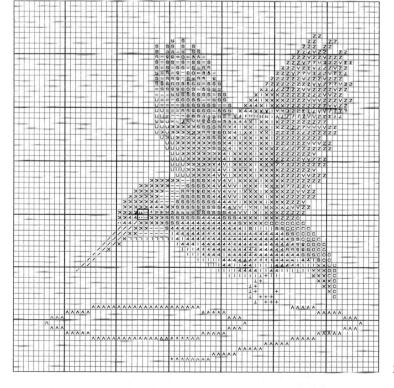

Stationery Set

This trio of useful items has been decorated with a selection from the wide variety of flowers to be found in fresh-water habitats, including purple loosestrife, yellow flag and water mint (often found together), plus cuckoo flower and water avens.

STATIONERY SET

YOU WILL NEED

For the address book, measuring 20cm × 15cm
(8in × 6in):

*53cm × 30.5cm (21in × 12in) of cream,
18-count Aida fabric
47cm × 16.5cm (18¹/₂in × 6¹/₂in) of white interfacing
Stranded embroidery cotton in the colours given in
the appropriate panel
No26 tapestry needle
An address book of your choice*

For the stamp book, measuring 9.5cm × 7.5cm
(3³/₄in × 3in):

*21cm × 10cm (8¹/₄in × 4in) of white,
14-count perforated paper
21cm × 10cm (8¹/₄in × 4in) of stiff white paper
for lining
Stranded embroidery cotton in the colours given in
the appropriate panel
No24 tapestry needle
51cm (20in) of green ribbon, 6mm (¹/₄in) wide*

For the telephone index pad, measuring
22.5cm × 8.5cm (8³/₄in × 3¹/₂in), with an oval
aperture measuring 8.5cm × 5.5cm (3¹/₂in × 2in):

*13cm × 11cm (5in × 4¹/₂in) of cream,
18-count Aida fabric
Stranded embroidery cotton in the colours given in
the appropriate panel
No26 tapestry needle
A blank telephone index pad, prepared for
embroiderers (for suppliers, see page 40)*

•

THE EMBROIDERY

For the address book, fold the Aida in half, giving you
a working area of 26.5cm × 30.5cm (10¹/₂in × 12in).
With the fold on the left, measure in 12mm (¹/₂in)
from the fold and baste from top to bottom. Measure
a further 15cm (6in) across and baste another,
parallel line. Baste two horizontal lines 20cm (8in)
apart and equidistant from the top and bottom edges
of your working area. This will leave a 20cm × 15cm
(8in × 6in) rectangle for the front cover. Place the
design towards the bottom left-hand side of the
rectangle, leaving a 1.5cm (⁵/₈in) margin on both
sides. Add two lines of basting stitches to mark the

position of these margins. Begin at the
bottom left of the chart. Use two strands of cotton for
cross stitches, and two strands for backstitching,
except for the insect, where only one strand is used.
Steam press on the wrong side when complete.

For the stamp book, using a soft pencil, draw a
line dividing the paper into two areas, each measuring 10.5cm x 10cm (4¹/₄in x 4in). This pencil line
will be the fold of the stamp book. Position your
embroidery so that the left-hand cross stitch frame is
approximately 7mm (¹/₄in) to right of your pencil line.
Working the frame first, stitch your embroidery,
using three strands of cotton for the cross stitches
and two strands of cotton for the backstitching.

For the telephone index pad, find the centre of
your piece of Aida, and start your embroidery from
the centre of the design. Use two strands of cotton for
the cross stitches and two strands for the backstitching. Steam press on the wrong side when complete.

MAKING UP THE ITEMS

For the address book cover, centre the interfacing on
the back of the Aida fabric. Fold the Aida to form a
narrow hem along all the edges, enclosing the interfacing, and machine stitch into position. Centre the
address book on the wrong side of the fabric and fold
the extra width over the free side edges of the front
and back covers. Seam along the edges at the top
and bottom to form pockets at the front and back.

For the stamp book cover, fold the perforated
paper along the pencil line to form the cover for your
stamp book. Fold your stiff lining paper in two and
carefully stick it in position inside your already folded perforated paper. Fold the ribbon along the spine
of the stamp book and make a bow on the front.
Books of stamps will slip inside and you can keep
them in place by slotting them through the ribbon.

The telephone index pad comes with all you need
to mount the embroidery and assemble the pad.

WATER AVENS TELEPHONE INDEX PAD ▶			
(Geum rivale)	DMC	ANCHOR	MADEIRA
6 Lemon	727	293	0110
▽ Dark green	3362	263	1601
– Bluish green	3363	261	1602
· Green	3347	266	1408
S Dull purple	315	1019	0810
T Purplish pink	3688	66	0605
U Pink	3689	49	0607
Dull pink*	3687	68	0604
Dusky pink*	223	895	0812

*Note: backstitch stalk of bluish-green leaf in bluish green; the flower
sepals in dull purple; the petals in dull pink*; the stalks of the dark
green leaves in green; the stalks of the dark green leaves in dark
green, and the flower stems in dusky pink* (starred colours are used
for backstitch only).*

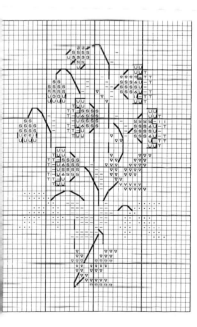

PURPLE LOOSESTRIFE, YELLOW FLAG & WATER MINT ADDRESS BOOK
(Lythrum salicaria, Iris pseudacorus & Menta aquatica)

		DMC	ANCHOR	MADEIRA
⊟	White	White	1	White
▯	Dark Brown	3031	905	2003
4	Yellow	725	306	0108
5	Lemon	726	262	0109
▽	Dark green	3345	268	1406
△	Green	3346	262	1407
+	Light green	3347	266	1408
·	Pale green	3348	265	1409
↖	Very dark green	3362	263	1601
→	Bluish green	3363	261	1602
↑	Light blue green	3364	260	1603
X	Yellow green	472	264	1414
⊓	Ginger brown	435	365	2010
L	Deep lilac	208	111	0804
Z	Lilac	210	108	0802
C	Pale lilac	211	342	0801
●	Deep pink	3607	87	0708
H	Pink	3608	86	0709
■	Pale pink	3609	85	0710
	Grey*	413	401	1713
	Dusky pink*	223	895	0812

Note: backstitch the fly's wings and legs, and the flower centres of the loosestrife in grey; the stems of the water mint in dusky pink* (starred colours are used for backstitch only); the fly's body, the lighter leaves of the loosestrife and the leaf veins of the water mint in pale green; the stamens of the loosestrife in deep pink, the leaf veins of the darker loosestrife leaves in light green, and the detail on the iris flower in ginger brown.*

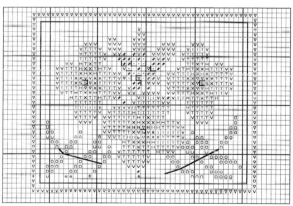

CUCKOO FLOWER STAMP BOOK ▲
(Cardamine pratensis)

		DMC	ANCHOR	MADEIRA
5	Yellow	725	306	0108
▽	Green	470	267	1502
O	Bluish green	3363	261	1602
·	Pale green	472	264	1414
⚡	Light green	471	266	1501
X	Cream	746	275	0101
V	Purplish pink	3608	86	0709
H	Greyish pink	316	969	0809
T	Pink	3609	85	0710
	Dark grey*	413	401	1713

Note: backstitch the leaf stalks in bluish green, the border in green; and the flower centres and detail at the base of the buds in dark grey (used for backstitch only).*

Bellpull and Bookmark

In the tall damp grasses alongside a river, the common frog finds food and shelter. The common damselfly also frequents the area, while in spring the mayfly emerges from the water and is often seen clinging to reeds or grass stalks.

BELLPULL AND BOOKMARK

YOU WILL NEED

For the frog bellpull, measuring 29cm × 10cm (11¹⁄₂in × 4in):

*43cm × 23cm (17in × 9in) of cream,
18-count Aida fabric
35.5cm × 15cm (14in × 6in) of cream lining fabric
29cm × 10cm (11¹⁄₂in × 4in) of iron-on interfacing
Stranded embroidery cotton and blending filament
in the colours given in the appropriate panel
No26 tapestry needle
Pair of metal bellpull hangers, 10cm (4in) wide*

For the frog bookmark, measuring 23cm × 7.5cm (9in × 3in):

*26cm × 11.5cm (10¹⁄₄in × 4¹⁄₂in) of white,
14-count perforated paper
26cm × 11.5cm (10¹⁄₄in × 4¹⁄₂in) of iron-on interfacing
45.5cm (18in) of green ribbon, 12mm (¹⁄₂in) wide
Stranded embroidery cotton and blending filaments
in the colours given in the appropriate panel
No24 tapestry needle*

•

THE EMBROIDERY

For the bellpull design, prepare the fabric by marking the centre lines with basting stitches. Begin stitching from the centre point on the design. Use two strands of cotton in the needle for all cross stitches, except where metallic thread is indicated. In this case, combine one strand of cotton with one strand of blending filament. For backstitching, use two strands of cotton, except for the detail on the insects' wings, where only one thread is used. Be particularly careful when backstitching over the wings, as it is very easy to catch and snag the metallic thread when bringing the needle through from the back of the fabric.

For the bookmark design, find the centre of the perforated paper by counting the spaces between the holes. Work the cross stitches first, using three strands of thread in the needle, except where metallic thread is indicated. In this case, combine two strands of cotton with one strand of blending filament. For the backstitching, use two strands of cotton in the needle, except for the detail on the insects' wings, where only one thread is used.

FINISHING THE BELLPULL

Centre the interfacing on the back of the embroidery and pin it in place. Remove the basting stitches and iron the interfacing into position. Trim the long edges until the piece measures 13cm (5in) wide. Turn in the long edges by 12mm (¹⁄₂in) and press. Trim the short edges until the piece measures 38cm (15in) long. On the two short edges, make a 6mm (¹⁄₄in) turning. Make a second turning 4cm (1¹⁄₂in) deep, taking the fabric over a rod at the top and bottom. Baste and neatly hem in place.

Turn in the long edges of the lining fabric and then the short edges, so that it will neatly cover the back of the work. Slipstitch in place.

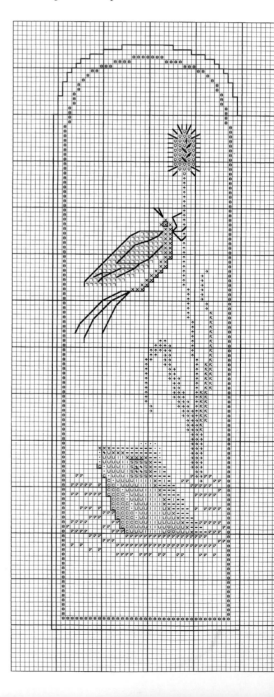

COMMON FROG, COMMON BLUE DAMSELFLY & MAYFLY BELLPULL ▶

(Rana temporaria, Enallagma cyathigerum & Rhithrogena)

		DMC	ANCHOR	MADEIRA
Z	Black	310	403	Black
⌝	Silvery grey	415	398	1803
	+ Kr. 001 (Kreinik silver blending filament)			
I	Dark brown	3371	382	2004
5	Gold	972	298	0107
◸	Light iridescent blue	775	128	1001
	+ Kr. 001 (Kreinik silver blending filament)			
·	Blue	597	168	1110
▬	Medium brown	610	889	2106
U	Fawn	612	832	2108
↖	Dark green	3345	268	1406
→	Green	3347	266	1408
↑	Pale green	3348	265	1409
C	Cream	739	885	2014
▪▪	Yellow brown	830	277	2114
T	Brown	3031	905	2003
X	Yellow	676	891	2208
I	Yellow green	734	279	1610
▼	Biscuit	738	942	2013
	Grey*	414	400	1801
	White*	White	1	White

Note: backstitch the frog's back leg in brown; the frog's throat and belly, and the Mayfly's body and tail in fawn; the insect's wings in grey; the line over the frogs eye in dark brown; the insects' legs and antennae in black, and the frog's eye highlight in white* (starred colours are used for backstitch only).*

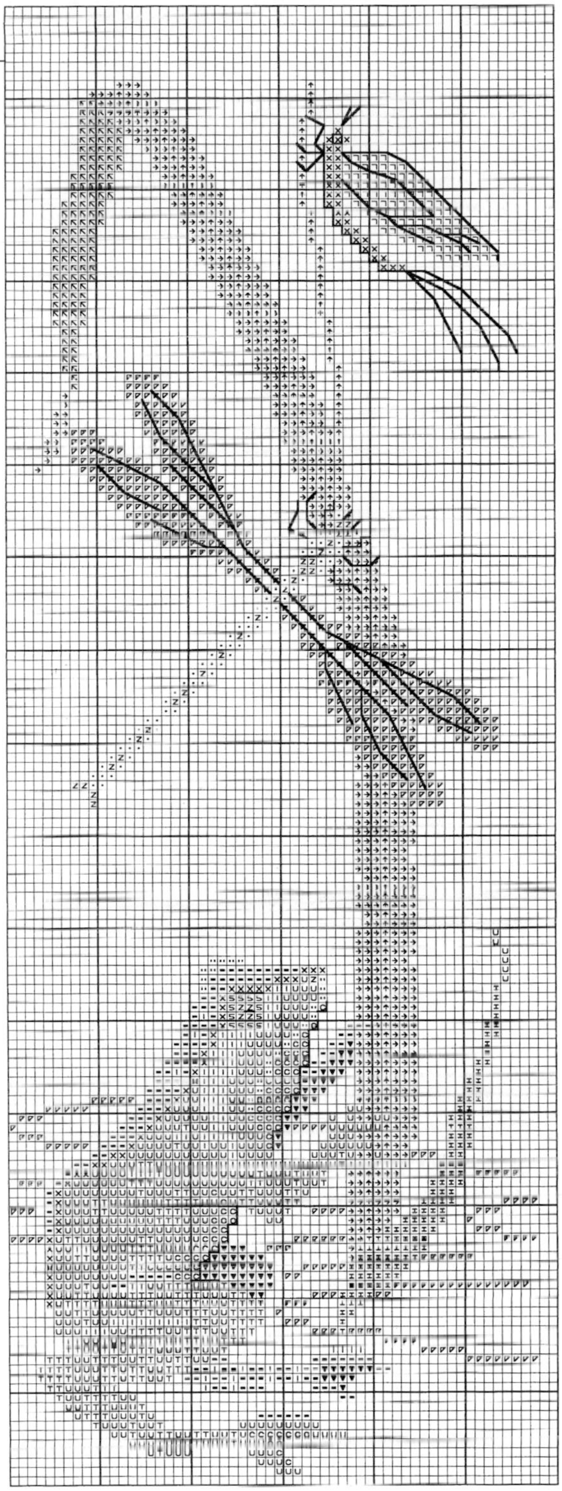

COMMON FROG & DAMSELFLY BOOKMARK ◀

		DMC	ANCHOR	MADEIRA
↘	Black	310	403	Black
⌝	Silvery grey	415	398	1803
	+ Kr. 001 (Kreinik silver blending filament)			
I	Dark brown	3371	382	2004
5	Gold	972	298	0107
8	Iridescent blue	518	168	1106
	+ Kr. 094 (Kreinik blue blending filament)			
◸	Light iridescent blue	775	128	1001
	+ Kr. 001 (Kreinik silver blending filament)			
▬	Medium brown	610	889	2106
II	Fawn	612	832	2108
↖	Dark green	3345	268	1406
→	Green	3347	266	1408
↑	Pale green	3348	265	1409
C	Cream	739	885	2014
·	Yellow brown	830	277	2114
▽	Brown	3031	905	2003
X	Yellow	676	891	2208
	White*	White	1	White
	Grey*	414	400	1801

Note: backstitch the seed on the reed seed head in brown; the frog's eye highlight in white; the frog's throat and the mayfly's body and tail in fawn; the mayfly's wings in grey* (starred colours are used for backstitch only); the line over the frog's eye in dark brown; and the mayfly's legs and antennae in black.*

FINISHING THE BOOKMARK

Centre the interfacing on the wrong side of the bookmark, then iron it in place. Trim around the border of the design, leaving an edging of two perforations. You may find it easier to mark your cutting line with a soft pencil before you start. Cut the ribbon in half. Gather along the edge of one piece and tighten it into a rosette. Fold the other length in half to make two streamers, and stitch the fold to the lower edge of the bookmark. Glue or stitch the rosette in place over the streamers.

Bird Studies

These two studies of nesting river birds are attractive as pictures or could be used for very special cards. The great crested grebe often nests on a floating platform of grass anchored among reeds. The moorhen also nests on a platform, using dried water plants close to the reed-fringed waterside.

BIRD STUDIES

YOU WILL NEED

For each picture, mounted in a frame 22cm (8³⁄₄in) square, with a circular aperture measuring 13.5cm (5¹⁄₂in) in diameter:

33cm (13in) square of cream, 18-count
Aida fabric
Stranded embroidery cotton in the colours given in
the appropriate panel
No26 tapestry needle
Strong thread for lacing across the back
when mounting
Stiff cardboard for mounting, cut to fit the frame
Frame of your choice

THE EMBROIDERY

Find the centre point of your square of material, and start your embroidery from the centre of the design. Complete the cross stitches first, and then the back-stitching. Use two strands of thread for both the cross stitches and the backstitching, except when outlining the eyes of the birds, when one strand is used. Gently steam press the finished embroidery on the wrong side.

ASSEMBLING THE PICTURES

Each picture is assembled in the same way. Trim the edges of the embroidery, allowing for a 5cm (2in) turning on all sides to fold over your cardboard mounting board.

Lace the embroidery over the mount, following the instructions on page 7, and complete the assembly according to the manufacturer's instructions.

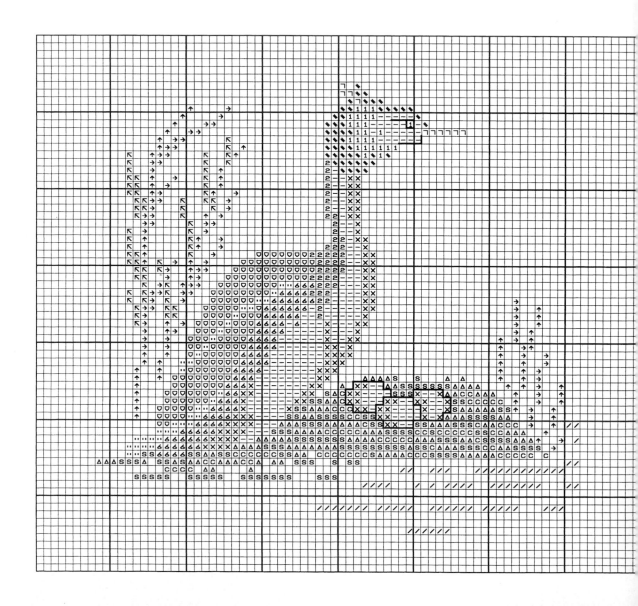

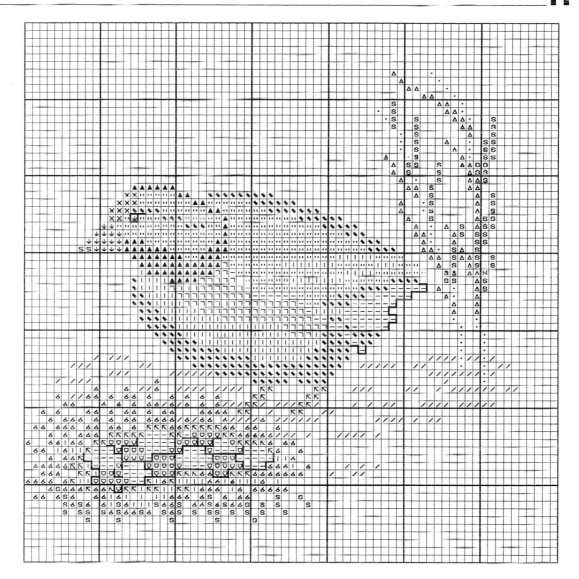

GREAT CRESTED GREBE ◀
(Podiceps cristatus)

		DMC	ANCHOR	MADEIRA
⊠	Black	310	403	Black
⊐	Grey	413	401	1713
☐	Cream	712	387	2101
1	Dull orange	920	339	0312
2	Yellow brown	420	375	2104
6	Reddish brown	300	352	2304
∕	Pale blue	775	128	1001
S	Dull green	3011	845	1607
△	Light brown	642	392	1906
C	Grey green	372	887	2110
↖	Dark green	3362	263	1601
⊐	Green	3363	261	1602
↑	Light green	3364	260	1603
⅄	Fawn	613	956	2109
❚❚	Dark brown	3031	905	2003
▽	Brown	610	889	2106

Note: backstitch the eye outline and the eggs in grey, and the grebe's throat in fawn.

MOORHEN ▲
(Gallinula chloropus)

		DMC	ANCHOR	MADEIRA
⊠	Very dark brown	3371	382	2004
⊐	Greyish brown	640	903	1905
⊟	Cream	712	387	2101
∐	Brown	610	889	2106
5	Yellow	972	298	0107
6	Grey green	372	887	2110
∕	Pale blue	775	128	1001
X	Red	349	46	0212
↓	Light red	350	11	0213
S	Dark green	3362	263	1601
△	Green	3363	261	1602
·	Light green	3364	260	1603
↖	Dull green	3011	845	1607
❚❚	Dark brown	3031	905	2003
▽	Fawn	613	956	2109
▲	Black	310	403	Black
	Grey*	413	401	1713

Note: backstitch the moorhen's tail in brown; the front edge of the nest in dark brown; the eggs in grey (used for backstitch only), and the eye outline in cream.*

ACKNOWLEDGEMENTS

I should like to thank my mother, Violet Watts, who made up or assembled all the embroidered articles illustrated in this book, and who patiently recorded the steps she took and the processes she employed for inclusion in the instructions for finishing the projects.

I should also like to thank Betty Haste for her help with the checking of charts and proofs at all stages of the preparation of this book.

My thanks are also due to Pauline and Anne of the Kaleidoscope needlework and craft materials shop, The Square, Codsall, Staffordshire, who have followed the progress of this book with such interest and have always been at hand with practical help and suggestions.

I should like to thank Len and Malcolm Turner of Fabric Flair, Warminster, Wiltshire, for the fabrics used in some of the projects in this book. I should also like to thank DMC for the fabrics and embroidery cottons they provided.

My acknowledgements would not be complete without a sincere 'thank you' to Ian and Martin Lawson-Smith of IL-SOFT, Specialist Craft Software, Witney, Oxfordshire, for their help and advice concerning the use of their excellent stitch design programme.

Finally, I must express my appreciation to friends and neighbours who followed the creation of these designs with such interest and gave me so much encouragement.

SUPPLIERS

The following mail order companies have supplied some of the basic items needed for making up the projects in this book:

Framecraft Miniatures Limited
372/376 Summer Lane
Hockley
Birmingham, B19 3QA
England
Telephone: (0121) 359 4442

Addresses for Framecraft stockists worldwide
Ireland Needlecraft Pty Ltd
2-4 Keppel Drive
Hallam, Victoria 3803
Australia

Danish Art Needlework
PO Box 442, Lethbridge
Alberta T1J 3Z1
Canada

Sanyei Imports
PO Box 5, Hashima Shi
Gifu 501-62
Japan

The Embroidery Shop
286 Queen Street
Masterton
New Zealand

Anne Brinkley Designs Inc.
246 Walnut Street
Newton
Mass. 02160
USA

S A Threads and Cottons Ltd.
43 Somerset Road
Cape Town
South Africa

Fabric Flair Limited
The Old Brewery
The Close
Warminster
Wiltshire
BA12 9AL

For information on your nearest stockist of embroidery cotton, contact the following:

DMC (also distributors of Zweigart fabrics)
UK
DMC Creative World Limited
62 Pullman Road, Wigston
Leicester, LE8 2DY
Telephone: 01162 811040

USA
The DMC Corporation
Port Kearney Bld.
10 South Kearney
N.J. 07032-0650
Telephone: 201 589 0606

AUSTRALIA
DMC Needlecraft Pty
P.O. Box 317
Earlswood 2206
NSW 2204
Telephone: 02599 3088

COATS AND ANCHOR
(also distributors of Kreinik blending filament)
UK
Coats Patons Crafts
McMullen Road, Darlington
Co. Durham DL1 1YQ
Telephone: 01325 381010

USA
Coats & Clark
P.O. Box 27067
Dept CO1
Greenville
SC 29616
Telephone: 803 234 0103

MADEIRA
UK
Madeira Threads (UK) Limited
Thirsk Industrial Park
York Road
Thirsk
N. Yorkshire, YO7 3BX
Telephone: 01845 524880

USA
Madeira Marketing Limited
600 East 9th Street
Michigan City
IN 46360
Telephone: 219 873 1000

AUSTRALIA
Penguin Threads Pty Limited
25-27 Izett Street
Prahran
Victoria 3181
Telephone: 03529 4400